Bible Beauty:
Adult Coloring Book

Grace Sure

What's Inside?

Bible Beauty: Adult Coloring Book – "One of the year's best adult coloring books".

Discover the beauty in the bible with this adult coloring book. 50 truly stunning images for you to color and enjoy. Inspiring Scripture quotes and beautiful designs, bring the beauty in the bible to life in glorious color. Gorgeous designs that range from simple to complex so you can produce works of art in minutes or hours

A coloring book that never runs out...

Buy the book today and you'll receive a link where you can print out as many copies of all the images as you want (great for sharing with your family and friends). Plus you can print out extras so you can re-color any designs you would like in new artistic ways....

You'll enjoy it - Plus Here's Why It's So Good For You -

The benefits of coloring have been widely reported. The Huffington Post reported "The practice generates wellness, quietness and also stimulates brain" they go on to say "In simplest terms, coloring has a de-stressing effect because when we focus on a particular activity, we focus on it and not on our worries". But it also "brings out our imagination and takes us back to our childhood, a period in which we most certainly had a lot less stress."

Extra Bonus

You'll also receive a wonderful free bonus of 10 extra images from my other adult coloring books.

Enjoy and Start Coloring Today...

"May the God of hope fill you with all joy and peace as you trust in him, so that you may overflow with hope by the power of the Holy Spirit."

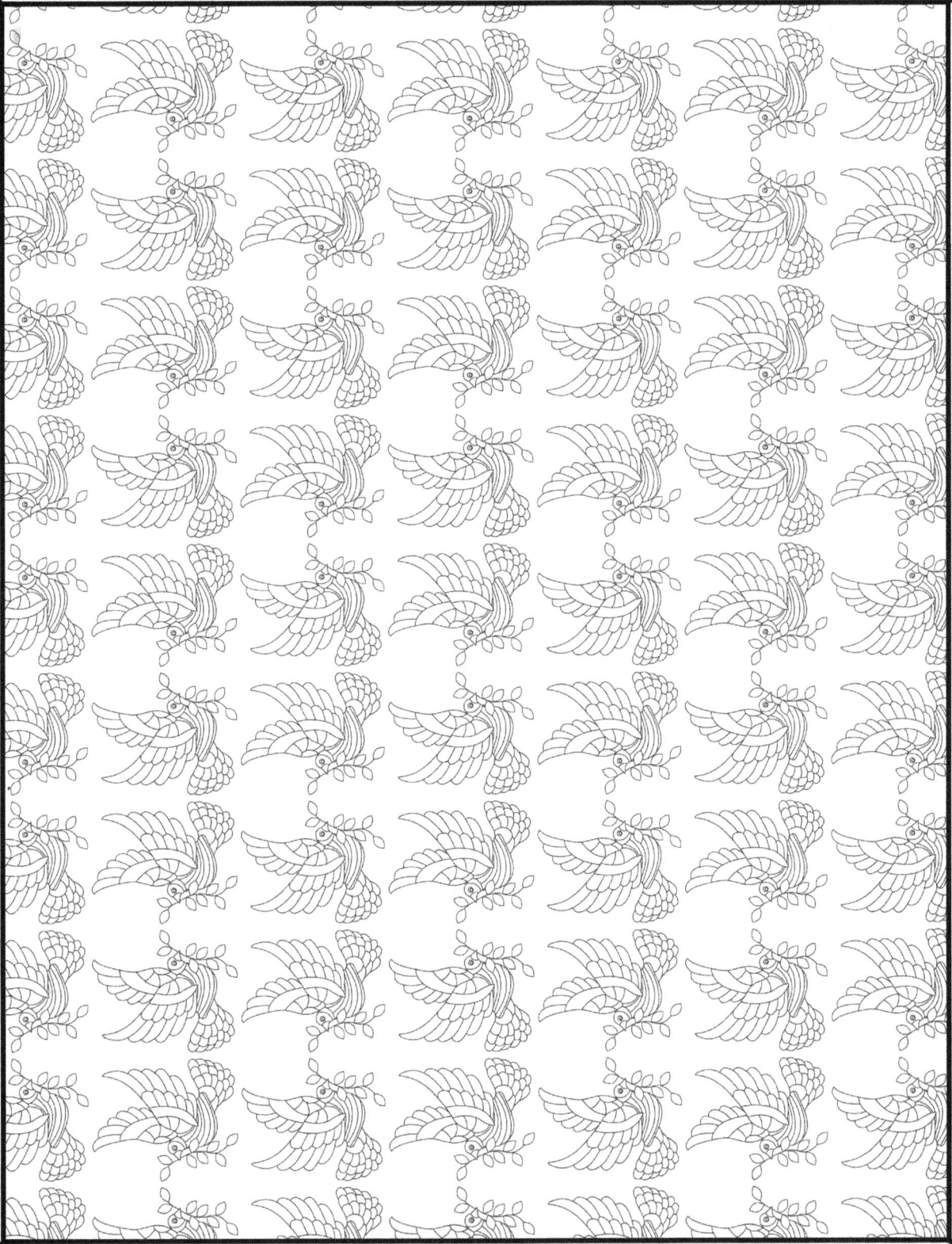

"Turn from evil and do good; seek peace and pursue it."

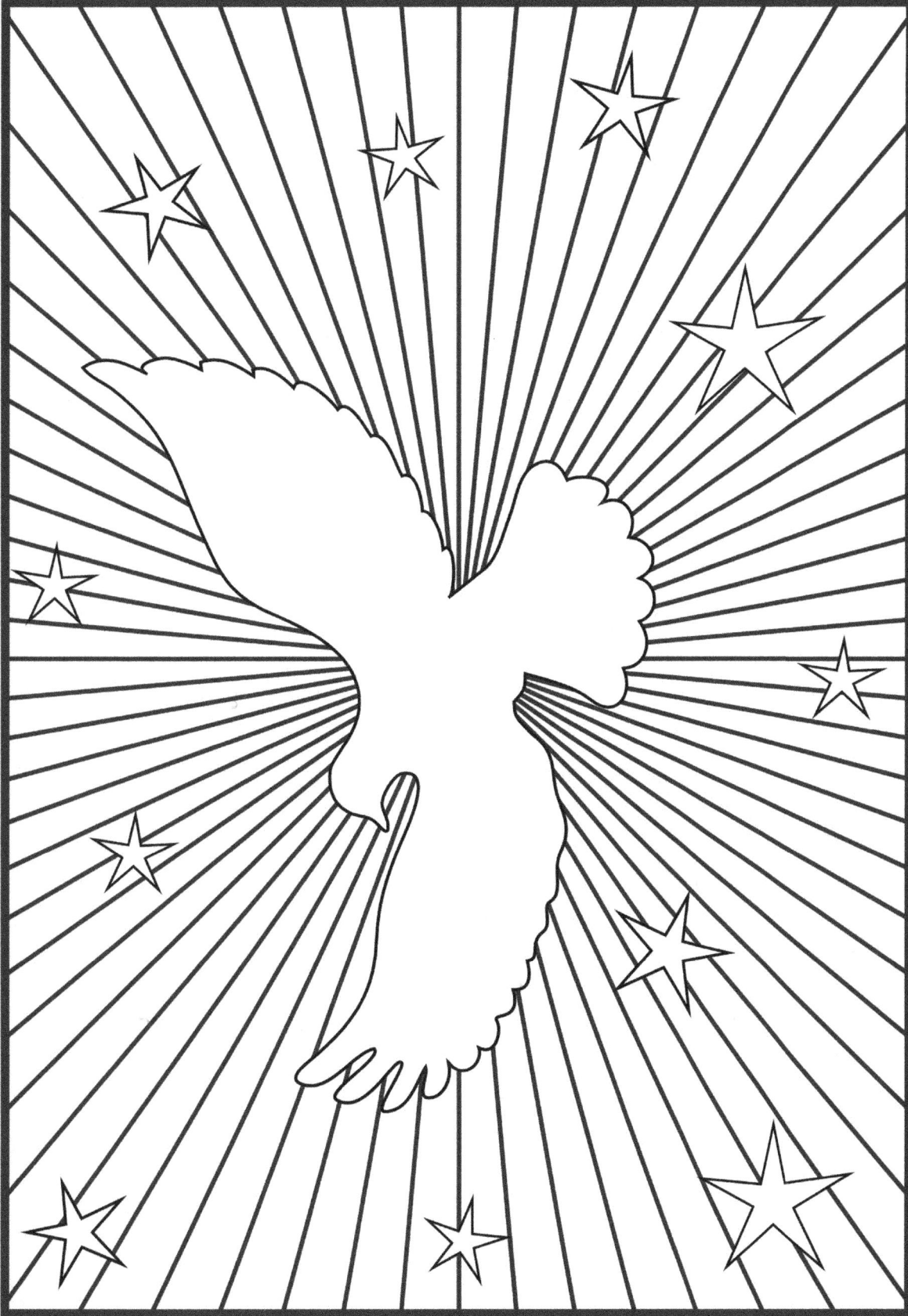

"The LORD gives strength to his people; the LORD blesses his people with peace."

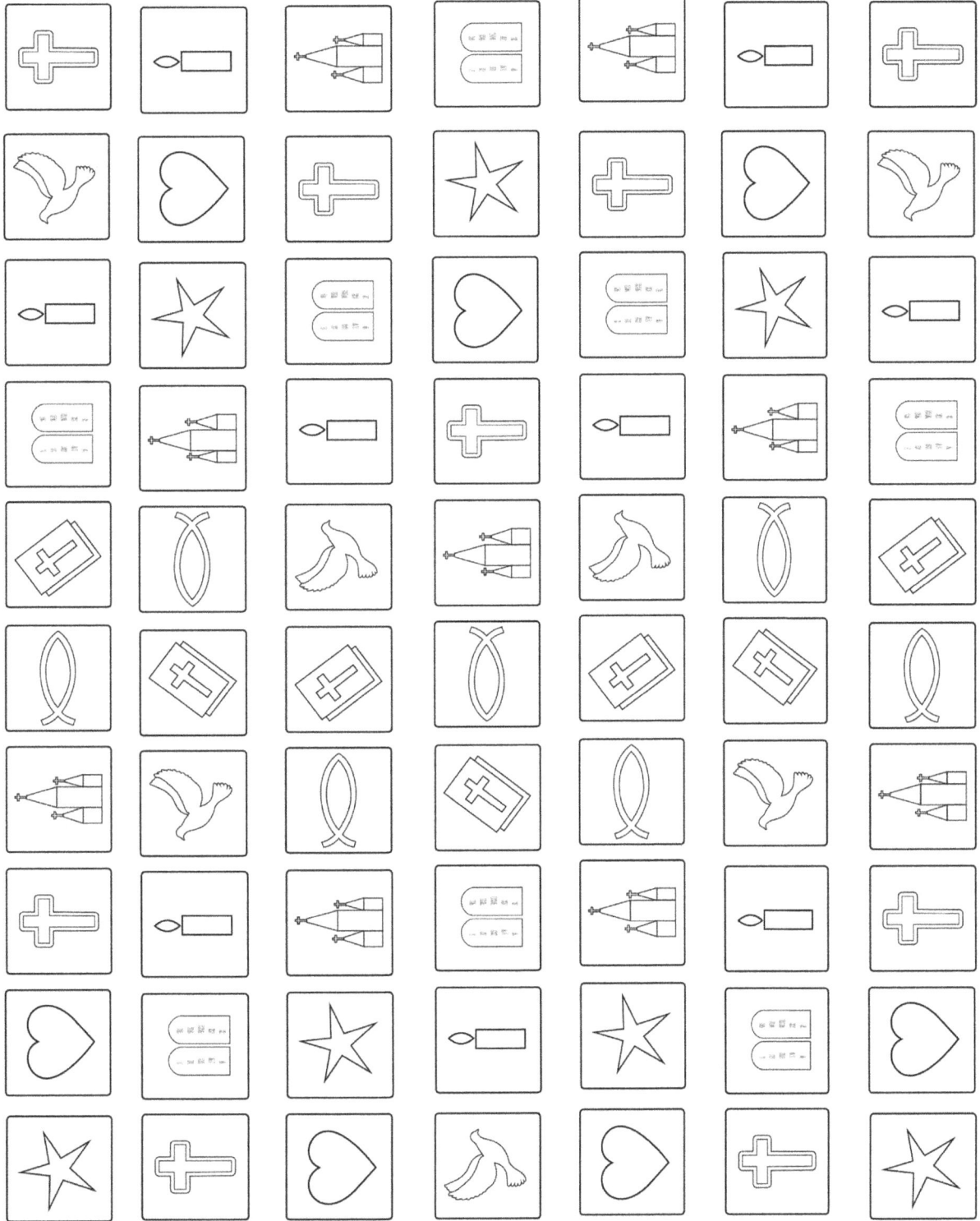

"God's love is like an ocean. You can see its beginning, but not its end."

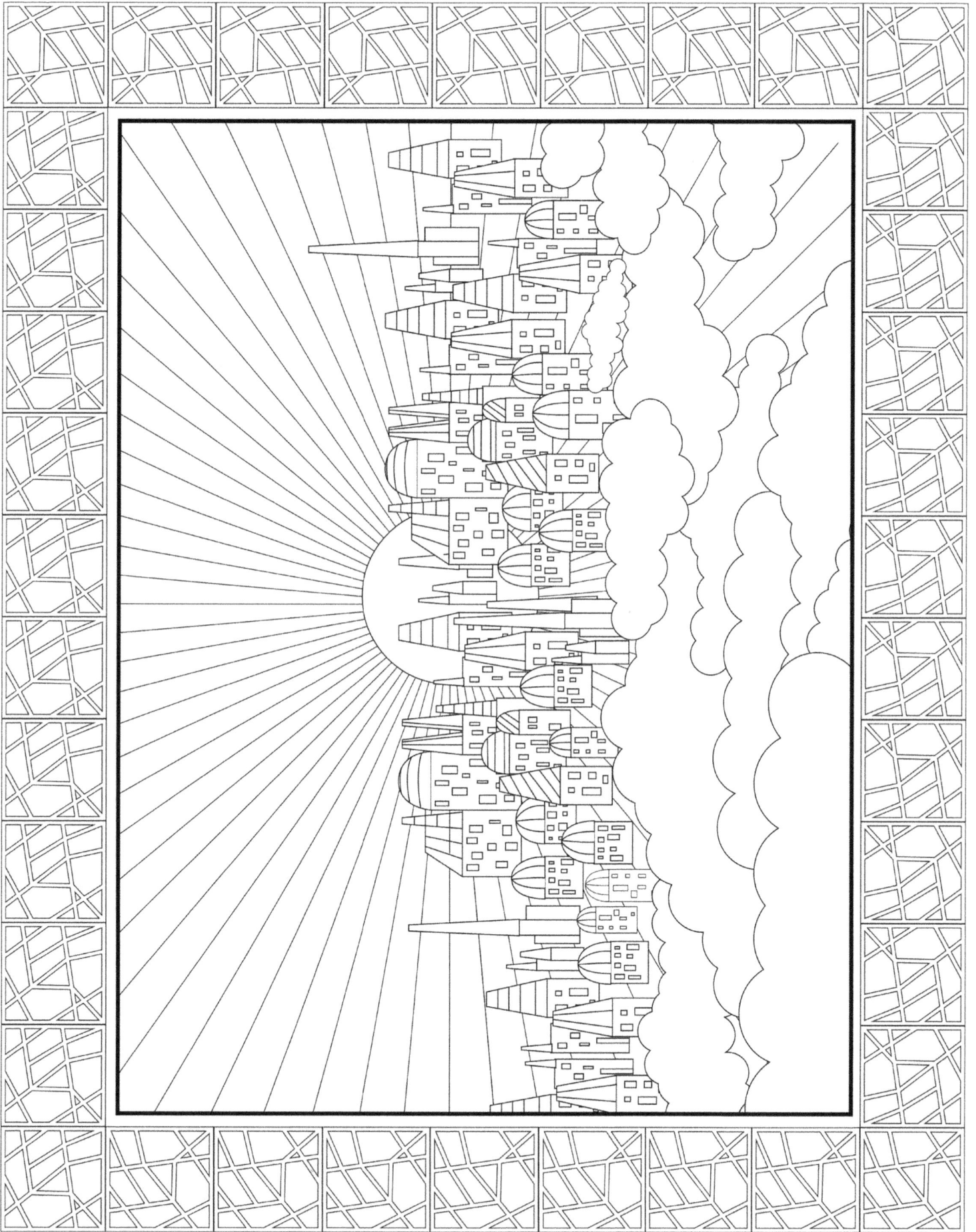

"For I know the plans I have for you, declares the LORD, plans for welfare and not for evil, to give you a future and a hope."

"For God so loved the world that he gave his one and only Son,
that whoever believes in him shall not perish but have eternal life."

"But the fruit of the Spirit is love, joy, peace, forbearance, kindness, goodness, faithfulness."

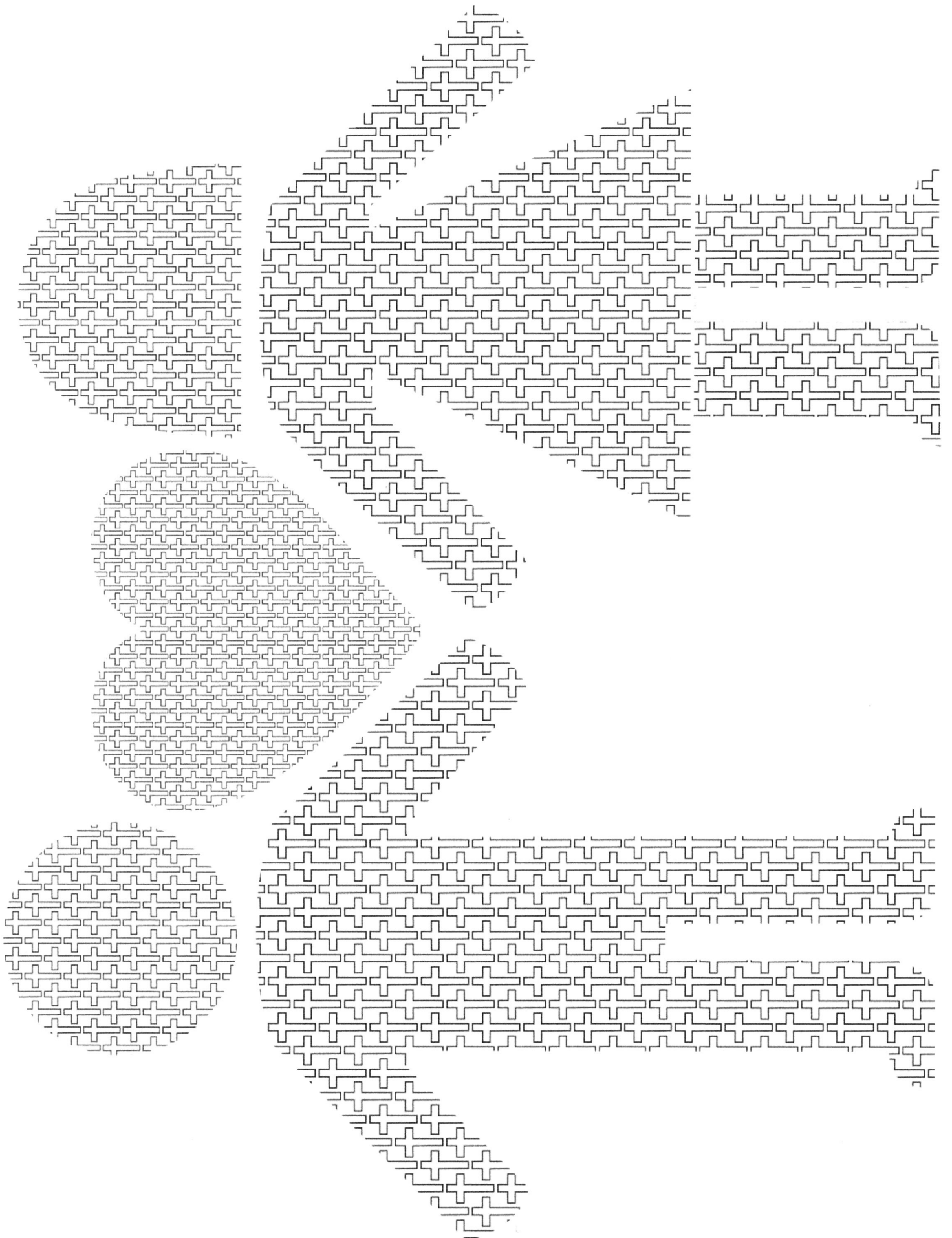

"Love is patient, love is kind. It does not envy, it does not boast, it is not proud. It is not rude, it is not self-seeking, it is not easily angered, it keeps no record of wrongs. Love does not delight in evil but rejoices with the truth. It always protects, always trusts, always hopes, always perseveres. Love never fails. But where there are prophecies, they will cease; where there are tongues, they will be stilled; where there is knowledge, it will pass away."

"Finally, brothers and sisters, whatever is true, whatever is noble, whatever is right, whatever is pure, whatever is lovely, whatever is admirable—if anything is excellent or praiseworthy—think about such things."

"Do not let your hearts be troubled. Trust in God; trust also in me."

"For I was hungry and you gave me food, I was thirsty and you gave me drink, I was a stranger and you welcomed me."

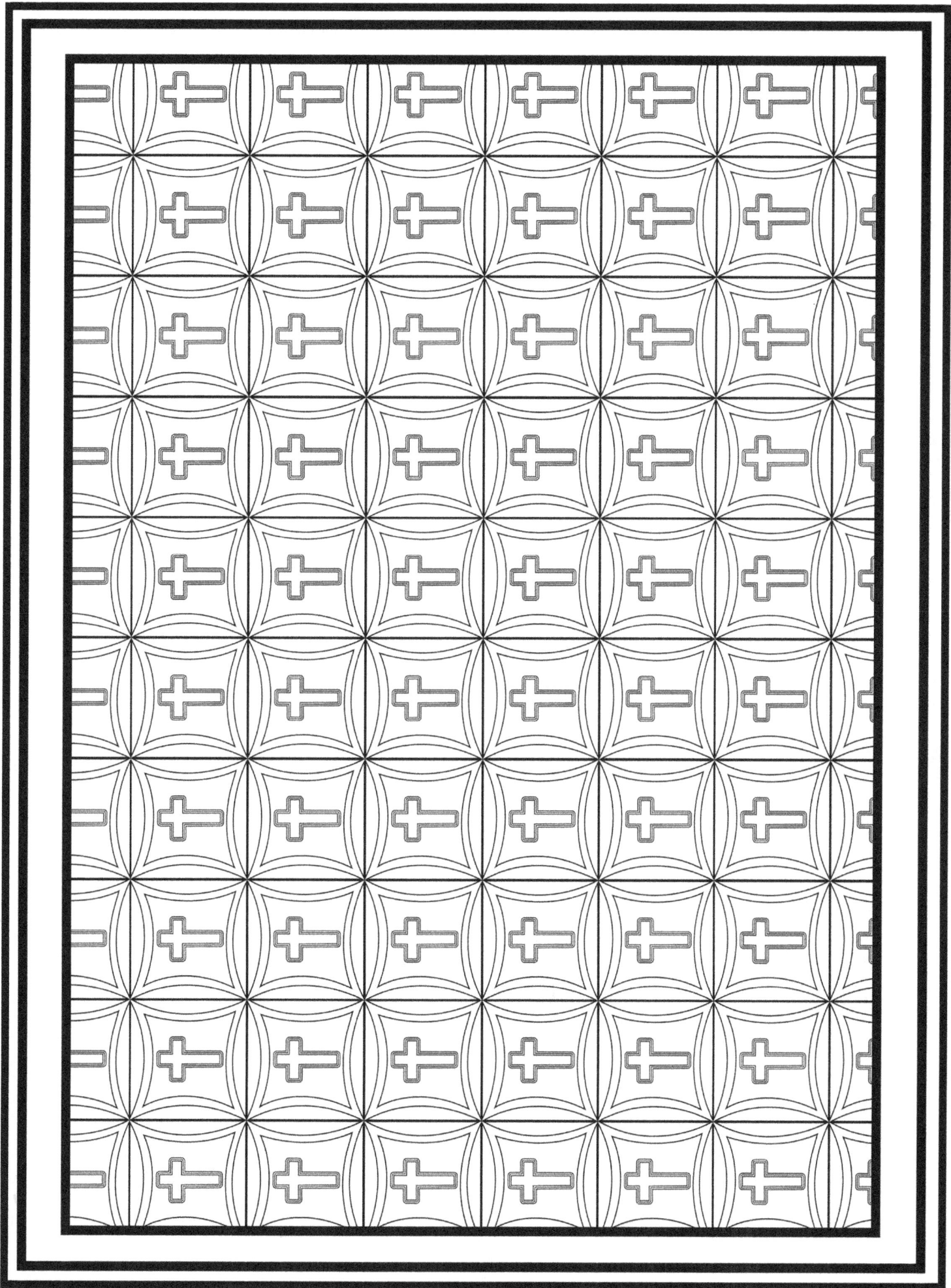

Enjoyed These?

Then you'll love our other beautiful detailed coloring books.

Over the next few pages please find images from some of our other adult coloring books.

If you like them please just search for them by book title (listed under each image) or by the ISBN online so you can enjoy the complete coloring book.

Other Coloring Books In This Series That You'll Enjoy

Paisley Coloring Book - Stunning Mystical Paisley Designs and Patterns
ISBN: 978-1-910085-84-4

All Our Adult Coloring Books
Coloring Books Designed for Artists, Adults, Teens and Older Children

Beautiful Birds

Bird Coloring Book Including Owls for Adults - Bird Paradise - My Beautiful Coloring Book
ISBN: 978-1-910085-74-5

Owls & Other Birds Coloring Book for Grown Ups: - On The Wings Of A Dove Coloring
ISBN: 978-1-910085-73-8

Cuddly Cats

Cat Coloring Book For Adults - My Captivating Creative Cat Designs and Patterns Artists Favorite Coloring Books
ISBN: 978-1-910085-30-1

Cats Coloring Book Creative Designs - Cute Little Cats Needing My Artistic Care
ISBN: 978-1-910085-29-5

Christmas Magic

Christmas Coloring Book for Adults - Fantastically Festive Patterns and Designs for Christmas Sparkle
ISBN: 978-1-910085-72-1

Christmas Coloring Book for Grownups - Santa and Rudolphs Classic Christmas Delights
ISBN: 978-1-910085-71-4

City Style

City Coloring Book for Adults - Fantastic Cities, Splendid Creative Designs
ISBN: 978-1-910085-70-7

City Coloring Book - My Secret City Creative Coloring Book for Adults and Older Children
ISBN: 978-1-910085-69-1

Doodling Doddles

Doodle Coloring Book to Color My Stress Away - Adult Art Doodle Coloring Book Enjoy the Creative Invasion!
ISBN: 978-1-910085-95-0

Doodle Coloring Books: - Relaxing Art Doodle Designs and Patterns
ISBN: 978-1-910085-94-3

Flower Delights

Flower Coloring Book for Adults - Beautiful Creative Floral Flower Designs and Patterns
ISBN: 978-1-910085-66-0

Nature Garden Flowers Coloring Book for Adults - Garden Flowers in Full Bloom in My Creative Designs
ISBN: 978-1-910085-65-3

Adult Coloring Book of Flowers - Bouquets, Roses, Garden Flowers a Creative Flower Coloring Masterpiece
ISBN: 978-1-910085-64-6

Geometric Magic

Geometric Coloring Book for Adults - Intricate Geometric Coloring Designs for Adults – Creative Color Your Imagination
ISBN: 978-1-910085-99-8

Geometric Coloring Book for Adults - Geometric Coloring – Book of Surprising Wonders
ISBN: 978-1-910085-98-1

Hippie Life

Hippie Coloring Book - Peace, Love and Hippies Coloring
ISBN: 978-1-910085-63-9

Coloring Book for Hippies - Relieve My Magical Hippie 70's and Feel the Love
ISBN: 978-1-910085-62-2

Love In My Heart

Peace and Love Coloring Book - My Beautiful Valentine Love Coloring Book with Gorgeous Designs
ISBN: 978-1-910085-61-5

Love Coloring Book for Adults - Creative Love of My Heart
ISBN: 978-1-910085-58-5

Mystic Mandalas

Mandala Coloring Book for Meditation – Effective Relaxation and Anti-Stress Mandalas
ISBN: 978-1-910085-90-5

Mandala Coloring Books for Adults - Coloring Creative Mystical Mandala Designs and Patterns for Relaxation and Meditation
ISBN: 978-1-910085-89-9

Mandala Artists Coloring Book - Beautiful Magical Mandalas to Color Today
ISBN: 978-1-910085-88-2

Mosaic Pieces

Mosaic Coloring Books for Adults - My Magical Mosaic Coloring Masterpieces
ISBN: 978-1-910085-87-5

Mosaic Coloring Fun Book - Creative Fun Mosaic Patterns and Designs
ISBN: 978-1-910085-86-8

Music Masters

Music Coloring Book for Adults - Color My Music, Fill My Passion
ISBN: 978-1-910085-52-3

Music Coloring Book - Love Music, Love Color
ISBN: 978-1-910085-50-9

Paisley Patterns

Paisley Coloring Book for Adults - Creative Coloring Paisley Patterns and Designs for Perfect Relaxation
ISBN: 978-1-910085-85-1

Paisley Coloring Book - Stunning Mystical Paisley Designs and Patterns
ISBN: 978-1-910085-84-4

Relaxing Patterns

Pattern Coloring Book - Detailed, Beautiful and Wonderfully Creative Coloring Patterns
ISBN: 978-1-910085-83-7

Adult Pattern Coloring Book - Modern, Detailed Artistic Pattern Adult Coloring Book for Relaxation
ISBN: 978-1-910085-82-0

Coloring Patterns - Unique Creative Pattern Masterpieces Designed for Artists
ISBN: 978-1-910085-81-3

Pattern Coloring Book For Adults - Color Me Patterns, Calm Relaxation Coloring Therapy
ISBN: 978-1-910085-80-6

Coloring Pattern Book - Imagination On Paper Coloring Patterns
ISBN: 978-1-910085-79-0

Spring / Easter Surprise

Headers: Easter & Spring Coloring Book - Creative Designs and Patterns for Adults and Older Children
ISBN: 978-1-910085-78-3

Spring and Easter Coloring Book - Hop Into Easter
ISBN: 978-1-910085-77-6

Sugarskull – Day of the Dead!

Sugar Skull Adult Coloring Book - Day Of The Dead Mexican Creative Sugar Skull Designs
ISBN: 978-1-910085-76-9

Sugar Skull: Dia De Los Muertos / Day Of The Dead - Coloring Book for Grown Ups
ISBN: 978-1-910085-75-2

Stained Glass Wonders

Stained Glass Wonders Coloring Book
ISBN: 978-1-910085-59-2

Tattoo Art

Tattoo Coloring Book: - My Creative Body Art Tattoo Designs
ISBN: 978-1-910085-44-8

Tattoo Coloring Book for Adults - Coloring Tattoos My Fantastic Body Art
ISBN: 978-1-910085-42-4

Wildlife Wonders

Wildlife Coloring Book - Forest Elephants, Giraffes, African Big Cats and More, Natures Wildlife Coloring Art
ISBN: 978-1-910085-36-3

Wildlife Coloring Book for Adults - Explore Wildlife in Natures Magnificent Animal Kingdom
ISBN: 978-1-910085-34-9

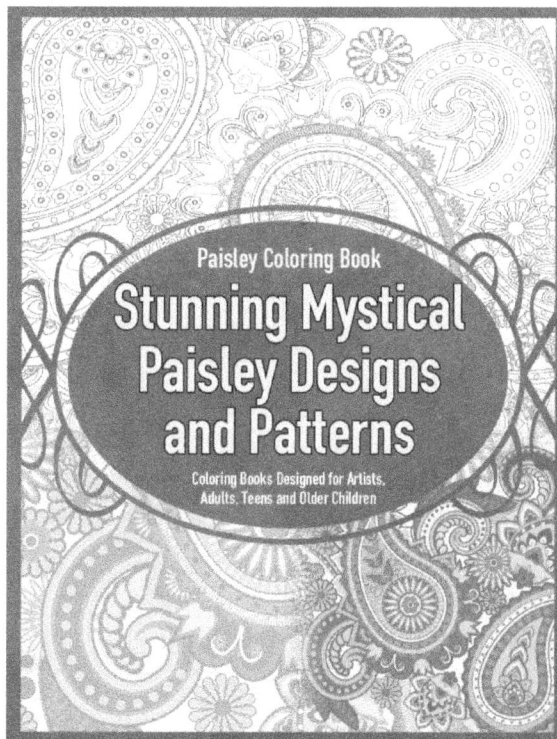

Paisley Coloring Book
Stunning Mystical Paisley Designs and Patterns
Coloring Books Designed for Artists, Adults, Teens and Older Children

FROM: Bird Coloring Book Including Owls for Adults - Bird Paradise - My Beautiful Coloring Book ISBN: 978-1-910085-74-5

From: City Coloring Book for Adults - Fantastic Cities, Splendid Creative Designs ISBN: 978-1-910085-70-7

Geometric Coloring Book for Adults - Intricate Geometric Coloring Designs for Adults Creative Color Your Imagination ISBN: 978-1-910085-99-8

From: Hippie Coloring Book - Peace, Love and Hippies Coloring
Coloring Books ISBN: 978-1-910085-63-9

From: Mandala Coloring Book for Meditation – Effective Relaxation and Anti-Stress Mandalas ISBN: 978-1-910085-90-5

From: Mosaic Coloring Books for Adults - My Magical Mosaic Coloring
Masterpieces ISBN: 978-1-910085-87-5

From: Pattern Coloring Book - Detailed, Beautiful and Wonderfully Creative Coloring Patterns ISBN: 978-1-910085-83-7

From: Easter & Spring Coloring Book - Creative Designs and Patterns for Adults and Older Children ISBN: 978-1-910085-78-3

From: Tattoo Coloring Book: - My Creative Body Art Tattoo Designs
ISBN: 978-1-910085-44-8

We also have a range of "Childrens Coloring Books"

ABC

Alphabet ABC Coloring Book - My First ABC and 123 Numbers Coloring Book
ISBN: 978-1-910085-32-5

Christmas

Christmas Coloring Book for Children - Santa's Magical Christmas Coloring Book for Children
ISBN: 978-1-910085-97-4

Christmas Coloring Book for Kids - Rudolph and Santa's Christmas Coloring Book for Kids
ISBN: 978-1-910085-96-7

Cute

Cute Animal Coloring Book for Kids - My Adorable, Cuddly and Very Cute Coloring Book
ISBN: 978-1-910085-68-4

Cute Coloring Book for Children - My Incredibly Cute Animal Coloring Book
ISBN: 978-1-910085-67-7

Dinosaurs

Dinosaur Coloring Book To Make You Roar!
ISBN: 978-1-910085-60-8

Halloween

Kids Halloween Coloring Book - Childrens Creative Halloween Coloring Books
ISBN: 978-1-910085-93-6

Halloween Coloring Book - Ghosts, Witches, Monsters, Haunted Houses and More... -
Art Halloween Books for Children
ISBN: 978-1-910085-92-9

Monsters and Aliens

Childrens Aliens and Monsters Coloring Book - My Crazy Monsters Coloring Fun
ISBN: 978-1-910085-56-1

Monster and Aliens Coloring Book for Kids - Monsters, Aliens and More Monsters Coloring
ISBN: 978-1-910085-54-7

Robots

Robot Coloring Book - My Monster Robot Coloring Fun For Kids
ISBN: 978-1-910085-48-6

Coloring Robots - My Robot Machines Fun Coloring For Children
ISBN: 978-1-910085-46-2

Summer Holidays

Kids Summer Holiday Fun Coloring Book - Perfect for Coloring on Childrens Car, Plane and Train
Journeys
ISBN: 978-1-910085-91-2

About Me

I have loved drawing from a very young age and now it is my pleasure to share with you a collection of my favorite images. I've spent months putting these together for you, I really hope you enjoy them. I have tried to include something for everyone, some with lots of detail others less for when you want to complete an image within a shorter time and with a wide range of images.

I hope you've enjoyed coloring these designs – Please can you help me?

Hopefully you've enjoyed coloring some or all of these images. Please, please, please can you take the time to share your thoughts and post a review on whatever site you purchased it from. It will be greatly appreciated and really help me – thank you.

Don't Forget

If you want to recolor any of these designs again you can and get more free images please just visit http://coloringfans.com/bible

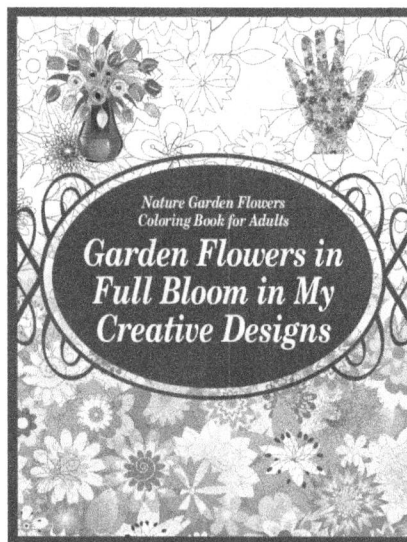

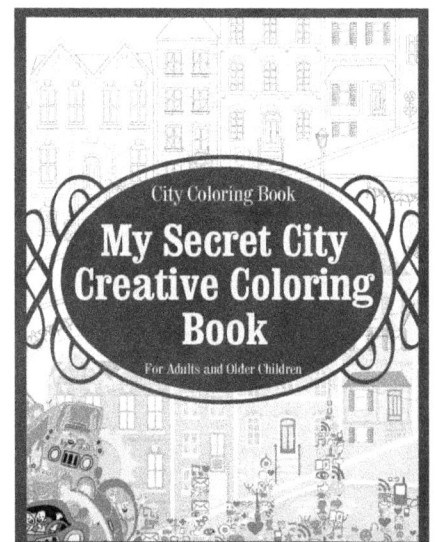

MORE FREE COLORING IMAGES...

Often when I release a new coloring book **I'll give FREE or Highly Discounted Copies to my previous customers**. If you are interested in receiving free copies just sign up below

Also...

Would you like to color some or all of these images in again? Perhaps in different colors or styles. Now you can print out as many copies as you like. I'll send you every design in this book free.

Please just visit
http://coloringfans.com/bible
so I can send you all the designs today.

Thank you so much for purchasing this book. I hope you have many happy hours coloring in all the wonderful images. As an extra 'thank you' I would like to invite you to join our free club.

I'll send you all the designs as a pdf document so you can just print them off at home as many times as you like - you can even print them for your friends, please just mention us. Just don't upload them online, sell them or claim they are yours!

Plus you'll receive advance designs of our new coloring books for you to enjoy free. If you'd like to 'show off' your skills I'm also putting together a gallery of your achievements. Details included when you join free.

http://coloringfans.com/bible
Please visit today

Thank you

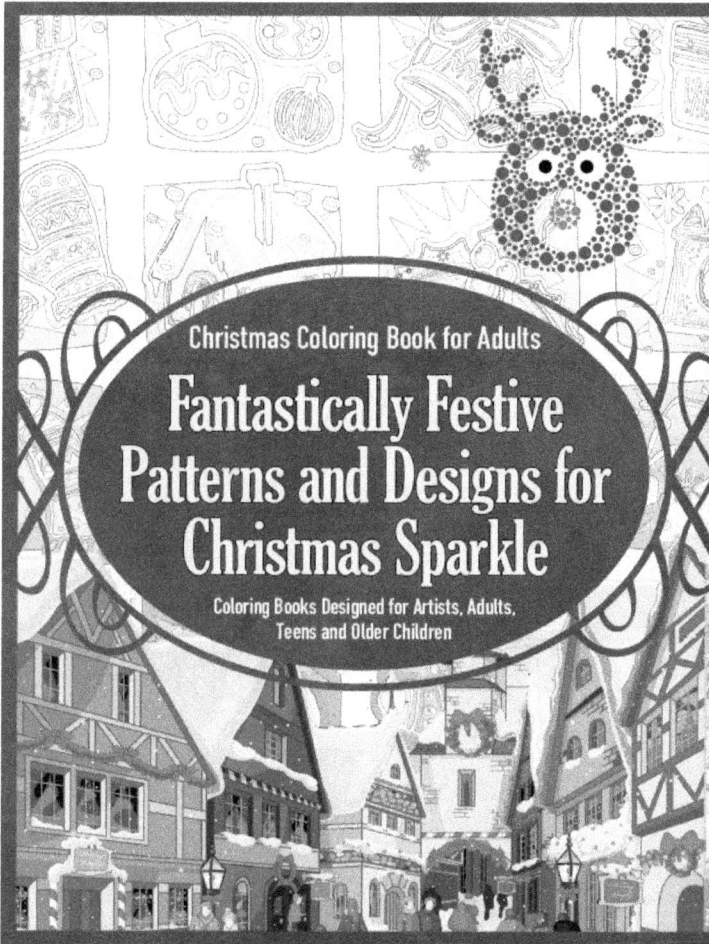

Christmas Coloring Book for Adults
Fantastically Festive Patterns and Designs for Christmas Sparkle
Coloring Books Designed for Artists, Adults, Teens and Older Children

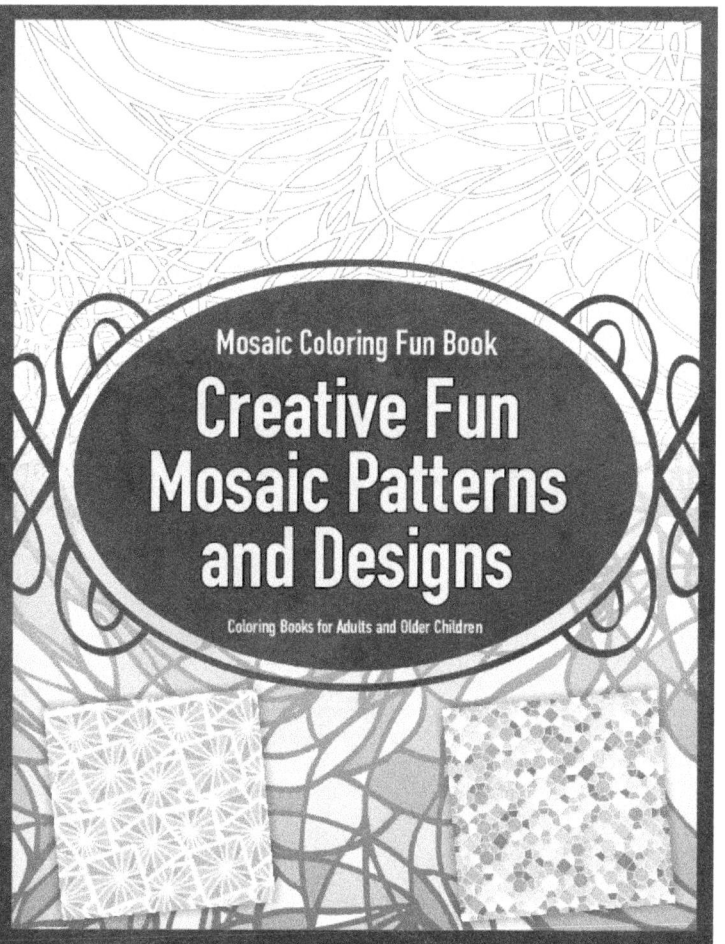

Mosaic Coloring Fun Book
Creative Fun Mosaic Patterns and Designs
Coloring Books for Adults and Older Children

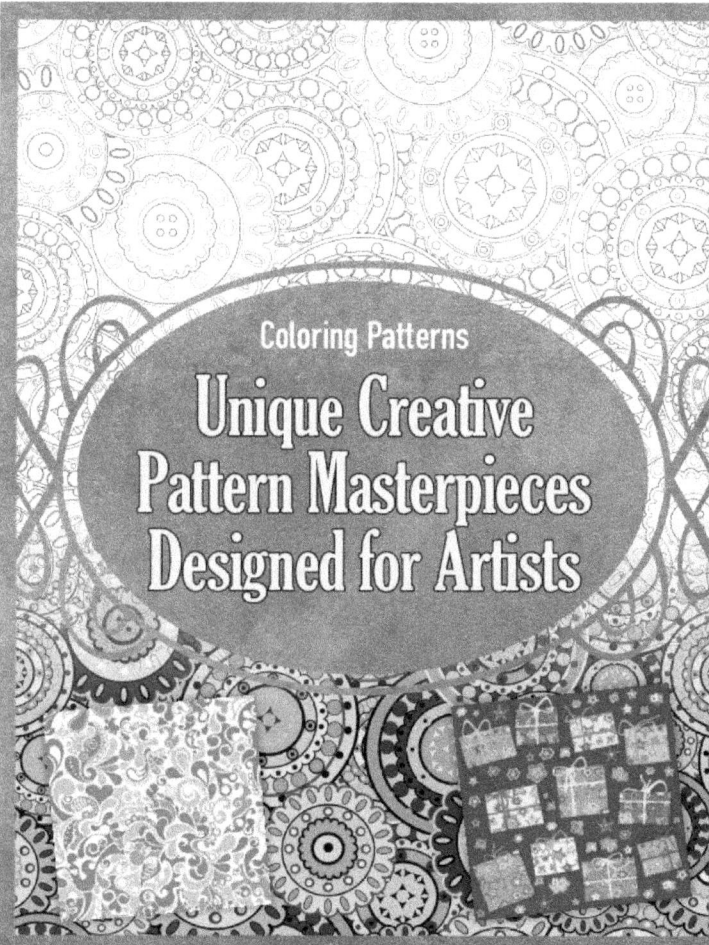

Coloring Patterns
Unique Creative Pattern Masterpieces Designed for Artists

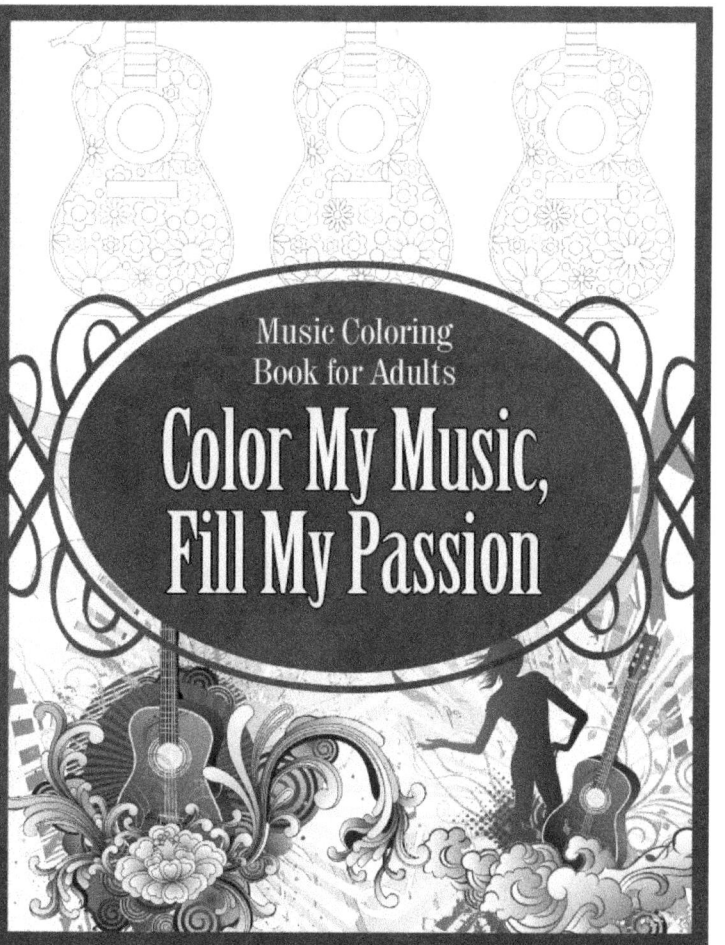

Music Coloring Book for Adults
Color My Music, Fill My Passion

www.ingramcontent.com/pod-product-compliance
Lightning Source LLC
Chambersburg PA
CBHW081213020426
42331CB00012B/3017